IF I WERE A CHICK...

By: Michael Lawrence

C-Me Publishing

1414 C-Me Dr.

Spring Lake, NC 28390

If I were a chick © 2014 Michael Lawrence. All rights reserved. 978-1-312-66800-3

AVAILABLE NOW IN STORES AND ONLINE

For more information on authors, contact publisher:

1414 C-Me Dr.

Spring Lake, NC 28390

631-394-1938

Acknowledgements

First I got to give thanks to God, he has showed me in many ways he does believe in me as I believe in him.

To my parents, I want you guy's to know without you, I would be lost. I want to thank my sister Lynisha and my Aunt Stephanie for all the support and love they given me.

My love I want to thank you for being you always and for reminding me every day, I can change my life. I want to thank you for reminding me; we can and will make it through all the rough times. I also want to thank you for never giving up on me and always know I will never give up on us. Love you!

Special thanks to my editor friend Jennah, she is a blessing. Thanks to her and her husband, Jeremiah, my novels will be typed and edited soon, so be on the lookout for "Tears of Joy" and "The Baldhead Murderer" Coming soon... until then I hope you all enjoy my character Chris Johnson and his version of self-help tactics.

With love,

Michael Lawrence

Dear Reader,

Don't take anything I say the wrong way. It's just my opinion on how I would do if I were a chick. In some ways you could say it's, how I would describe my perfect chick. So throughout this book you will read my view on things as if I were a chick. For the women it's a way to understand how one man thinks. From me, you can take what you want and use it how you like. I want the young women to see what a man sees when he looks at her. I want them to know what they already know but hear it and understand the effects it causes. What I believe is, if women change how they think about certain things, then our children will grow up with different values. Again I want to stress this is simply my opinion and I directed this toward no one.

Chris Johnson

Table of Contents

- Prologue
- Chapter 1: Appearance
- Chapter 2: Attitude
- Chapter 3: Men
- Chapter 4: Friends
- Chapter 5: Family
- Chapter 6: Goals
- Chapter 7: Independence
- Chapter 8: Keeping your man...
- Author's notes

Prologue

Everything is easier when you are looking at it from the outside. To men it's simply no reason why a woman shouldn't be able to keep her man happy. As men we feel like it's only a few things we concern ourselves with; sex, money and family. The problem with women is they like to make things harder than what they really are. For example, men I'm sure you came home from work very much so tired and your lady friend assumes because you don't want to have sex, your cheating. For some of you guys, yes you were cheating, but for those who really came home tired, they shouldn't have to pay for other peoples mistakes. Women, you like to get answers now. Which is fine, but some of you will do anything or say anything to get answers. This book is designed to show women how to handle serious relationship issues without looking like crazy girl Sally. This book is designed to give women the respect they deserve by teaching them how to earn it. Why should any man respect you when you don't respect yourself? To get respect you must earn respect. In this new day and age, society teaches us that being naked, is sexy and sexy is beautiful. Well I'm here to tell you the sexiest females I seen had clothes on. The art of the mind is beautiful if you want to know the truth. Knowledge is beautiful; the way God created the world is beautiful. What women don't realize due to TV is that most men will rather have a woman they could trust verses a big butt. What I mean by that is why I wrote this book. I want to express what I would do if I were a chick and honestly I hope it reaches some of the young women out there who act so grown up. I want them to stay young forever. When reading this, don't take anything personal, this isn't about you. It's about women losing themselves to keep a man happy who will never love them the way should be loved. It's about women lying down and accepting any and everything men throw at them. It's about me seeing my two daughters growing up knowing everything they should know, good or bad. It's about women learning their role and playing their part but mastering the art of your mind. See ladies when you can be happy with yourself, then and only then will you be able to master your own mind. It always starts with you, so allow me to show you, how to change you by changing how you think. Cray Cray I know but trust me ladies.

If I were a chick…

Sexiness isn't about an outfit, a hairstyle, how your make-up looks or how you walk. Sexiness is about your inner confidence.

-J. Miller

Chapter 1

(Appearance)

Let me start by saying, my name is Chris Johnson. I'm a fairly young dude and I have been through a lot, seen a lot, so understand I have done a lot. I was raised around nothing but women. There are more women in my family than men. I've watched the things women did and said. I made it a point to always listen and not speak. I knew at a young age, women had a lot to say and I could learn from listening. When I look at females, I notice things differently than most men. While you are looking at her breast, I noticed her teeth. A women's smile means so much more to me. When you watched her ass walk by, (I did too) but I was looking at her feet. It's something about a women's foot area that makes me decide whether or not I'm interested. Most men would say something like. "She was sexy." I'm wondering why she didn't do her hair and nails. The mind set of most men is simple; they only see women as sex objects until they actually get to know whoever she is. Before actually knowing a female most men only think cute face, body and is she willing. Me on the other hand I'm looking for so much more. Let's pretend I was slightly cute, I would already feel like I could get any women I wanted. So I wouldn't settle for anyone who was offering the cookie so easily, so to speak. I would want the one no one could get, the one that cleared the room. My female would have to be top notch, to me. If I were a chick, I would make a man wonder what he had to do, to be with me. I would make every man that pass me wonder what it would be like. They would wonder because I wouldn't reveal too much. I wouldn't be the conservative type; I would be more like up to date with fashion but less provocative. As a female your style is everything. How you dress yourself, will tell a story within itself so dress well I should say. If I were a chick I would show my figure some but not too much. The point would be to give the little people something to think about. My shoes would be essential; I wouldn't have to have the best, just simply the freshest. My shoes would never be dirty, as a female I would understand my foot area will attract attention always. Dirty shoes or feet, will never be attractive. Some female don't understand how to wear certain shoes at what time. I would dress for the occasion meaning if I'm just going outside to the store, I would wear sneakers. If I was going to a friend's house I would wear flats or sneakers. My point is I would never step out like I'm going to the club when I'm only going to a cook out. I would want people to approach me correctly so I would dress the way I would want to be treated. I would want respect and I would get it. When a female wears clothes that are revealing, it invites people to stare or even speak. Some men will go as far as touching a female as she walks by. The problem, was one, he was wrong for touching her but two she made him feel like it was cool since her ass was out for him to touch. As a female you control how people react to you. If you looking like a slut bucket than chances are some man will treat you like one. Women I need you to understand; this is true for married and single women. Your foot area is important whether you trying to keep a man or trying to get a man. If I were a chick I wouldn't wear a lot of make up if any. I understand some women need to wear makeup whereas others can make it look so beautiful on them. If I were a chick I would prefer my natural self. When it comes to hair I believe it should always be natural. When you start mixing and dying your hair it loses its texture. Natural is usually the best for most things. No weave no extensions, no wigs, just saying if I were a chick I'd go all natural.

Appearance would be important to me. Not so much of what other people thought about me but more like how I view myself. I would set high standards for me. I would want to be the best at whatever I did so I would dress the part. I believe in dress for success and things will happen. My opinion is if I were a chick I would understand my appearance stands out. It speaks for me without my permission. It gives off vibes that I can't control. Knowing these things I would control my appearance to appeal for me. I would make it work for me. The type of life, friends and or job I want would show from my appearance. I would own it and be proud of how I look. Remember when doing so, you will attract people however you look. Make sure you are attracting your type by dressing right. In every stage of appearance you will find your creeps. It's how you handle those situations that will define you later in life. As women you should understand your something like gold. Every man wants it, we don't need it we just want it. So when a woman understands that she plays a major part in every man's life, it's like winning the lottery. I would understand that I don't need a man. If I were a chick I would truly understand how life goes. In life a man needs a woman to plant his seeds. Every man that is worth any damn wants to be loved. I would see through the bull shit and lies. If he truly wants to be with you he will show it in the way he does things. He would rub your feet even when he really doesn't want to. He would go out his way to show you he cares. So when it comes to creeps, just let them go. There is no need to waste valuable time with someone who will never be what you want. Let's be honest ladies, what you want is exactly what you want. There's nothing wrong with that as long as you understand no one is perfect. With that being said you may find what you're looking for but he will have his flaws. If I were a chick I would understand this fact. I would know that my man will make mistakes. I would understand if he is truly the one for me, I could forgive him when he's wrong. This goes both ways though ladies, if I were a chick I would expect my man to understand I may have flaws also. No one is or will ever be perfect but two people with the right harmony can be perfectly happy together. My point is if I were a chick I would understand the power my appearance held. Control how you look first then you can begin to control how others view you.

In *__The Greatest Secret Untold__* I had explained how appearance is everything. I want men and women to understand what I mean. We can't control how the world changed or what the world has become only God can. One thing I know is, the people, and they have a different view on everything. In our world, appearance is the key to success. Make sure you choose the right path for the roads you want to travel. Respect yourself and the world will follow. If I were a chick, I would show the world who I am, through my skills and talents verses my attributes. Again, understand I don't hate the game. I just wish women could view themselves through a man's eyes and see what we see.

Chapter 2

(Attitude)

A lot of women would have fewer problems if they corrected some things involving their appearance. With that being said if I were a chick I would assume, I would have to show less aggression. I say this because when you look at certain people whose appearance is a lot less sexy, their attitude shows less. I wouldn't have to worry about KeKe and Laquisha because I wouldn't be in their league. Females feel threaten by other females that are within their circle of men. If I were a chick I wouldn't involve myself in circles that weren't in the area of goals I wanted to achieve. So pretend I'm a model and we all know there is so much competition out there. If I was this type of female I wouldn't be the model on the news all the time. I would be the one you seen but never heard about. As women, you have to set boundaries, and always stick to them. If my life wasn't going how I wanted it to I would understand, it's me that's causing everything. As people period we need to know everything's starts with us. I say this a lot but you have to change you first then begin changing your life. My attitude would be pleasant because I am happy with myself. When people approach me, I would smile and kindly speak. If I were a chick I would be soft spoken but my words would come out very clearly. If I had a problem with another female I wouldn't cause a scene. I would be the type to pull you to the side and speak to you. As women it's not cute to be loud all the time. It's not sexy to be the loudest person in a room. If I were a chick I wouldn't like too much attention. I would rather just know I look good verses everyone in my face. I would never be the life of the party. Some men love that but as for me I wouldn't want to be the party girl. I would want to be somebodies friend, someone's lover. I would want the people around me to know I'm secure about me. I would have the winning champs smile. Your personality defines you, it's your character. I would choose my character smartly if I could. Depending on what you want out of life, there's certain ways to handle yourself. No matter which way you do it, understand you get what you put into it. I wouldn't be a stuck up chick. Men don't respect that; the men I know wouldn't even look twice at them. Even if I had money I would never act like I'm better than anyone. To me, it's a straight turn off. I see lots of women more concerned about how they look than they are worried about their kid's behavior. Children are a reflection of us so if your kids see you acting one way, they will assume its ok. Again, to change you, you must change how you think. If you can't see anything wrong with your attitude, how will your child understand what's wrong? The way women handle problems with men should be something a young child never knows. Try not to argue around children; try to keep them out of grown folks business. If I were a chick I would make it a point not to do certain things in front of my children. If I smoke I would smoke in areas I know my child wouldn't visit. If I was a drinker I would conceal my drink. See were talking about how you think now. When you think differently from how you usually would the people around you will notice. Even if your child knows you smoke, the fact you smoked away from them, teaches boundaries. If I were a chick, I would adjust my attitude to inflect the message I was trying to present.

So tell me...

1. What does your attitude say?

2. Are you the stuck up type?

3. Can you understand if you think one way the people closest to you will associate you with those thoughts?

4. You become how you act, so what do people see you as?

Chapter 3

(Men)

Handling men should be easy for all women but we know that's not true. Most women wonder what to do and how to do it when it's much easier. As women you should understand men should do what you want. In a sense, you're his rib so he would do anything for that rib. If I were a chick I would know what I like and then understand what I want. Women can like one thing but truly want another. When you understand and love you, all that becomes one. So naturally you will find a guy who is everything you dream of. Until then you continue to focus on what's important in your life. Men are everywhere so I wouldn't carry my day worrying about getting a man. If I were a chick I would let him come to me. When he does I wouldn't be aggressive or stuck up. I would smile and politely have conversation if he was my type. Now if I wasn't interested I would kindly send him on his way. Men get nervous too, so it takes a lot for some men to approach women. I wouldn't be rude but I would send him on his way. If I were married and I was out with my girls, I would let them do the talking. When it comes to men, if you speak they will speak. Meaning no matter how many times you tell someone your married if you speak one time, a man will take that has he may have a chance. That's if he's really into you. Some men like to chase married women just saying. So if I were a married chick I wouldn't converse with men. When they came around I would surely keep it moving. It's something about the male species, they don't give a hoot. If you wink you will fuck. I would watch the things I did around men. In most cases I would separate myself from men when my husband wasn't around. If I were a single chick, I would speak to those I thought was my type. We all know we don't get it right the first time. We should learn ourselves first then choose who we like. Women need to realize if you take control and stop accepting anything from men, they will in turn learn they need to change something about them. When a man really wants you and truly loves you he will take that extra step for you. That's what you want. You want him to realize who you are; you want him to be the man you want. To do that, you have to make sure you are playing your part, meaning make sure you are what he wants. Don't think or guess if it's you he wants. You must remember if he wants you he will do what you ask of him. Don't be a slave owner because no man likes a women who wants to change him or likes to give orders. If I were a chick I would make sure my man knows the difference between what I need and what I am asking of him. Some women don't know what they want from a man. All they know is, they want a good man who is down for them. When they need to realize it's you men want. It's you the men talk about. So when you understand this, you begin to see new things you didn't see before. Look at it like this, men do what you allow. Therefore stop allowing just anything to happen to you. When you establish certain boundaries they will not be crossed if you enforce them. You have been allowing men to say and do anything they want, that's why he talks to you like he does. If I were a chick the moment some guy talked crazy to me, I would correct him. Then I would make sure I didn't give him the satisfaction again. I wouldn't look his way or speak to him. Why? Because I want things to go my way and when they don't I should be able to stop everything and move on.

My point is when it comes to men all women needed to know is, if you take control of you, you will notice the change in the men who flock to you. I don't want women to think I'm bashing I just want women to see what I see. I'm hoping women will think about themselves more and we could see our daughters grow up stronger than us. If I were a chick I would remember I am the beginning of life and I control what happens to me. Everything starts from within, remember that. Be happy with you first, it's the most important. Once you have a hold on you, that's when you step out and get the man you deserve, a man who is within your standards. I would never try to become what any man asks of me. He would and will be happy with me for who I am. Trust me when I say there is a man for every woman in this world. What women need to do is, stop trying to be what a man wants you to be, and start being who you want to be. As a man I can truly say it's was the women who had there things in order that had me watching. I never liked a chick that would be so aggressive that I have to say stop. That type of chick will never have any respect from a man. She will forever be a jump-off. Like I said before if you want to change how people look at you, you need to change how you think about you first. Men are simple, just be you and the one you want will come.

Let me know...

1. Could you let a man go after he proved not to be who you thought he was?

2. What if you were with a man for years and nothing changed the way you wanted, would you stay?

3. Could you go into every relationship you have, knowing you control the outcome?

Chapter 4

(Friends)

Friends are a different story, it's not having friends its more about the friends you have. Most men will and always will believe friends of a feather flock together. If you have a friend that is a little loose, most men will think you are loose too. Now understand me, when I say I feel you ladies but men will never think anything other than what they believe. Meaning if your friend is a hoe they will think you are too. That's when you choose your friends wisely or you separate yourself from them. This is for those who are looking for more in life other than the club. Married women became married for a reason. Females think playing a certain role in titles them something special. It's not the things you do or the way you do them, its how long and how consistent you are. For example, if you came through and cleaned my house for a week, don't expect me to think you wifey material when I don't even know you. If I were a chick I would understand this man. I would know exactly who and what I was dealing with. When I put myself in a man circumference I would already know what I'm doing. I wouldn't want my dude to know how Shonda got down. I would understand Shonda is the reason why people think you all easy. Who wants to be label as easy? Imagine it's you looking at your girlfriend and she all dressed up sexy as hell then here walks in Shonda. "Girl is you ready?" It's automatically a problem for women because every man will be skeptical. I would keep my friends, "My friends" and my personal life separate. I would want the relationship to grow first. It's possible for a female to be around a straight slut bucket and not be just as her friend. It's just hard to prove to any man. It takes time to make a man understand and know you are different than the rest. Your friend's whether you know it or not, they define you in some way. If I were a chick I would be aware of the company I kept. This isn't high school, so build up a strong relationship with your man before you go introducing him to friends. I'll keep this one short and sweet but understand what I mean. Your friends will define you so you can hate it, like it or love it but own it.

Just asking...

1. Do you have a friend that everyone says is easy?

2. Do you define your friends or do they define you?

3. Friends, how many of us have them? LOL

Chapter 5

(Family)

To me family is very important. I grew up in a big family of women so I've seen and heard a lot. The one lesson I learned about family is they should always have your back. In most cases this is never true. Sometimes it's your family who stabbed you in your back. What I want to talk about is the family that's sticks together. My family wasn't the best but I thank God for each and every one of them. For me family has been the back bone of my success. When I had nothing and needed my family most, they were there. When I did the dumbest things, they were there. Whenever I needed someone to talk to, they would sit on the phone and listen. I've had those moments in life where all I needed, was someone to pray for me and my auntie would say "Let's pray" I thank God because he blessed me enough to live and love my family. For these reasons and more, I understand how important it is to have a loving family support. I understand there are many people out there who will never know what I mean. I also understand it's too many people out there who want to feel the same way. Most people want to have a family of their own. Most men have certain values and morals when it comes to family. I know some women who never speak to their family. I have seen sisters fight each other over men. I saw two brothers fight over a women. Some females do not like to be around other females. It's a fact that females have certain dominance in them. Territorial is another word I could think of. Every family has its problems. That's for sure but it's how the family handles those problems. If I were a chick I would of course be a family girl. I would hope that my family respects whatever it was I did. If I had my own family, meaning home, kids, and husband or live in boyfriend; I would do what's necessary for them. I would respect my husband when it came to my appearance. I wouldn't allow my children to see anything I wouldn't want them to do. I would have to live to be the example. I would understand as a woman my appearance affects the family. My attitude would have to remain at a certain level. I wouldn't turn up until it was necessary and only for my family. Then again I may turn up for other reasons if someone got out of line but that's not the point. Stress is 90% of all the drama filed problems women have. Most women like drama, they are attracted to it. As a man I want women to know I hate drama. I run from it, I don't want to argue with you or anyone else. Let's get to the point...I don't speak for all men. If I were a chick I would want to be married, I would want someone to love me. I would believe family is important and I would want a family. I'm sure every woman does but it's not easy for everyone. We are so worried about what we want we sometimes forget about what's important to us. I would do my best to keep my family together and happy. Coming from such a family orientated background, I would want my children to have the same values I was raised with. I would teach my children respect by showing them respect. I would make sure the people around me respected my children also. I'm not saying women should live and do things how I'm saying. I'm just telling you ladies what I would do if I were a woman. I would understand that the things I did around my children will affect them. I wouldn't show off my body if I had children because it would send the wrong message to my child. Women should realize when it comes to girls; they watch their mothers but listen to their fathers. So if I were a chick I would make sure my daughters knew how a woman should be. It would take more than me telling them so I would show them. I couldn't be the mother out there in the streets talking about people and starting fights. I wouldn't be the mother who was out there in the streets sleeping with different men. I wouldn't be the one who slept with married men either. I would have to show my daughters the mother they deserve. I would be a major part of their lives; I wouldn't rush them to grow up. I would never leave them for a man. Some woman do dumb shit, I would try not to be one of them. To have a baby and have nothing to do with your child is crazy to me. Men do it all the time but it's something I would expect. Coming from someone who grew up with only a mother I know how it feels to see your mother doing everything. If I were a chick I would be just like my mother when it came to being single. No matter what she went through she made a way for us. She never let us feel her struggle, when she may have been. It was the strength she processed when the time called for it. See to her, family was the most important thing so she did what she had to. If I were a chick I would understand how my family was important to me so I would maintain myself accordingly.

Intrigue me...

1. Do you have kids?

2. Would you consider yourself the family type?

3. Do you want to have a family of your own?

4. How far would you go for your family?

Chapter 6

(Goals)

When you ask some women what goals do they have in life, it's amazing to hear how many still have no idea. If they do know what their goals are, some won't take the time to achieve those goals. For all you women who know what your plans are in life, this isn't about you. This is about the women who need to get up and start making things happen. As always I must start by saying to accomplish goals you have to first want to do it. You want to have a passion for whatever it is you're trying to achieve. Once you have an idea of what you want to do, you have to make it happen. Failure is an option so continue to strive at all cost. I'm not saying everything will change or happen for you overnight no. I'm saying if you take the time to try first, then something may happen. If it doesn't work your first time around, try again but in a different manner. We tend to give up too easily and that's people in general. When you want something badly trust me most of the time you will get it. Meaning want your goals badly and you will achieve them. No matter how big or small your goal is, when it's important to you, you should believe in yourself enough to achieve anything. If I were a chick I would break my goals down to short term and long term goals. For instance, my short term goal would be something like becoming the manager where I work. My long term goal would be to eventually own my own business. For me to do these things for one, I would have to be very active at my current job if I want to be manager one day. I would have to put in any necessary work i had to, just to show my bosses I deserve more. When I got myself focused on doing something I would make sure I got it done. As far as my long term goal, owning my own business, I would take any necessary steps I had to. Meaning going to school at night or if I had to work two jobs, I would. I would understand if I want something in life I would have to go get it myself. As women, you should pride yourself on your work or your knowledge of your work. Never let a man or anyone in a position of power, use you because you are a woman. If I were a chick I would know how to talk to people. I would know how to divert anyone's attention from what they want to what I'm actually talking about. Women need to understand the power they have over men and other women. You have to know you and all your strengths. Learn yourself then take action accordingly. Your long term goals may seem long indeed but trust me if you have your mind focused and not afraid to fail and try again, I say you are in good shape. A lot of women need to stop being so lazy and start making things happen. You say you want this and that but do nothing to see it happen. Let's not be undecided, let's have a plan and see it through. The government is only helping but so much. I'm sure every female wants to be better or to have more. I don't see any reason why females shouldn't have all they ask for. If it was up to me I would give all mother's the world because I believe they deserve it. Well... the ones who are real mothers doing any and everything for the benefit of their kids. I respect those mothers, but even those moms will try, some women will never try anything but social service. As I said before you have to change your mind set. If you want more, better or just to do something about you, then start caring about you. Have more respect for yourself or your kids. Wouldn't you like to say I tried everything for mine and now that I have it I feel great? You should feel great, because when you achieve those goals you set forth, you learn something about you. You learn you can do anything you set out to do. With that feeling you become more powerful within you. First, write your goals down, short term and long term then take all the necessary steps to achieve them. Remember you can never give up, you must finish everything you start. Nothing good is ever easy so yes it will be hard. Just focus on what's important to you and you will be fine.

Tell me...

1. Do you have any goals in life?

2. What are some of your short term goals?

3. What are your long term goals?

4. Could you change some things in your life for your kids? Have you?

Chapter 7

(Independence)

To be independent is a beautiful thing. No matter male or female, everyone would love to be independent. When you have been depending on everyone but yourself for so long I can understand how it could seem hard. Women are very strong, I will say it, and I think women are a lot stronger than men. The problem is most women do not realize that fact. They accept things the way they are. If you ever want things to change, you have to change some things. Let's pretend no one will help you with anything, ever. Naturally you would grow an instinct for your survival. To be independent is exactly that, you have to think like no one in this world will help you. So everything will become your responsibility and your problem. Single mother's do it all the time so it can be done. Certain females need to grow up and become women. Childish women live childish lives with childish people. Remember this when you are learning how to better yourself. For those women who are happy with themselves and truly can say they are where they want to be then, again this part is not for you. I want to speak to the women who believe they will make a change without changing themselves. I want some women to realize if no man ever helps you in life always remember you have you. Independence comes from within; most females think because they have money, they are independent.

Let's look at the definition; Adjective

1. Not influenced or controlled by others in matters of opinion, conduct, etc.; thinking or acting for oneself: An independent thinker.

2. Not subject to another's authority or jurisdiction; autonomous; free: An independent businessman.

3. Not influenced by the thought or action of others: Independent research.

4. Not dependent; not depending or contingent upon something else for existence, operation, etc.

5. Not relying on another or others for aid or support.

6. Rejecting others' aid or support; refusing to be under obligation to others.

7. Possessing a competency:

By definition, are you Independent?

Not many will be, my point is; if I were a chick I would own my independence. To do that I would first, have to know where I was going in life, I would already have my goals in order. I would demand my independence by making it happen, so "Doing" verses "Talking about doing". What makes certain women independent is how they go about things. Independent women become so focused that they might forget to ask for help when they really need to. It's more than money, independence is a way of life, it's your mind set. Lots of people have money and still they don't have their independence. Independence is a freedom from all but one's self. To be independent become an independent thinker which means think about yourself for yourself. It seems easier to say then actually do but it's not. It's as I told you before when a female takes the time to be happy with herself for herself, everything I been saying will fall in place, as you want it to. Remember it's your life so do the things that will make you happy first, then love doing for others.

Ask yourself...

1. Are you independent?

2. What makes you feel independent?

3. If you are not independent, how do you plan to take back your independence?

4. How does it feel, to have control over you?

Chapter 8

(Keeping your man)

First let's start by asking is this the man for you? When dealing with men, you have to make sure he's what you want. Never the other way around, do you want to settle for anything? You have a choice when it comes to men. Once you believe and know he's the one for you, you should do what's necessary to keep him. Women have a lot of complaints when it comes to men. For one, you would have no complaints if you were happy making him happy. When you decided he was the one, right then you are telling yourself, this will work. Let's back up because some ladies still think they can make a bad situation turn good. You could never change him before and you never will. Stop trying to change a man just change the man you with. You want him to be someone else when you should be with someone else. Now if you have things in order, meaning if he's the one for you, then keeping him will be on your terms. If I were a chick I wouldn't worry about keeping a man because he would have to worry about keeping me. Some women act like they know what they want but really they don't. To keep your man, you must know what you want from him. You have to tell him before things get serious. There should be no surprises, make sure if you want a family you let him know in the beginning. Don't let him lie to you, be aware of his facial expressions, his body movements, and watch his eyes. All I'm saying is women lose a lot of men because of "The Things Changed Talk". She says "Things has changed, nothing is like it was before. " That's because here you are in a relationship with a guy you barely know. You have to base your relationship on something. If I were a chick I would base a lot off honesty and loyalty. I would need my other half to be both of those things. In the beginning of most relationships both qualities are concealed very well. I've learned to give someone opportunities early on to found out what I need. They say God wouldn't give someone patients; he would give them opportunities to be patient. Therefore I would test his honesty, but you must already know the truth. I would put him around other females alone to see if he could be loyal. I wouldn't send women after him, I would just be aware when other women were around just to see how he does.

If I were a chick I would understand my man. I would know how to keep him smiling, and know how to make him mad. I would have learned my boundaries with him and being that he's the man for me, I would respect those boundaries. After you realize a man is doing everything he could for you, sometimes you need to do everything you can for him. Ladies you have to know your man, meaning if he's mad at the world you should already know if he can handle it on his own or if he needs you to tell him it's ok. Sometimes ladies you should already know if he will take his anger out on you. Learn your man and you could avoid many problems in the future. So when asked how do I keep my man, I would say if I were a chick, it's all about two people learning and loving each other. Of course there will be moments when everything goes wrong, but it is how you handle those moments. This isn't really about keeping your man it's about women learning to love and deal with their man. If I were a chick I would know he loves me. When I see his bomb ticking, I would know to stay away. Sometimes ladies men don't want to talk about what's wrong. They want to sit there and figure it out themselves. When he's ready to talk he will come to you, never push an issue. Men need to be men but we want our women to be women. Strong women know when to be silent and when to speak up. Learn when it's your turn, so to speak. Women control the house-hold; remember to control your man by letting him be a man. If he's the one let him be the one, you just continue to be happy for you so you can be his back bone when he needs you.

My point is if you really want to keep your man it should be because you want to keep him. If you want to keep him, I say you do whatever you have to. Be happy first but keep your man if he's worth it. Real women keep their man because they listen. They know what to do and how to do it and that's only because they have learned their man a long time ago.

Learning your man is the key to keeping him.

"A lot of women think they know him but I'm sure they don't. Take the time to learn your man. "
-Michael Lawrence

Learn how your man operates.

There's only one question to ask.

1. Do you want to keep him?

   That's the only thing that matters and if you do want to keep him, I suggest you try accepting him for who he is and you continue to strive for you.

Author's Notes

When waiting for my novel to be edited, I grew bored and impatient. So I decided to write **The Greatest Secret Untold**, but after that my novels were still in the editing stage so as I'm promoting my first book, the females would ask, what about a book for women? It took me some time to concept an idea but when I did form ideas I wanted to present to women something they could read and understand how men think. I felt as if I could tell it like men say it is, and then women could see for themselves, what about them, should be changed. If any changes is needed at all. I just want the women in our world to look at them first, be happy then put everything else together. Ladies I hope you take from this book self-reinsurance. Be who you want to be today, stop waiting for a man and start making you happy now. As always I enjoyed sharing my thoughts with you, please be sure to check out my novels.

Lulu.com or Facebook/Michael Lawrence.

C-Me Publishing 631-394-1938

Michael Lawrence

IF I WERE A CHICK...

By: Michael Lawrence

Preview of my next novel

The Baldhead Murderer

For an old school kind of guy, Martin thought for sure he had everything planned out. He made sure no one saw him come in or out of his apartment building. He made sure to park his car in the same place every time. He always made it a point to park next to the street lights so he could look out the window and see his ride. Knowing the feds was watching his every move, he made it a point to leave his TV and the lights on, as he made his way to the basement. In the hallway he was nervous, he wasn't sure of which way to go. He looked both ways before he entered the next hallway. With no one in sight he kept moving swiftly but mindful of the open areas and windows. Martin stops and looks at the elevator then thought twice about it. "Maybe they have someone looking to see if the elevator stops or leaves my floor" he thought so he proceeded towards the stairs. As he descended at each level he would listen first, then look, then move. He wanted to be sure he was *getting away clean. He had enough money to last him a lifetime and nothing in his way, but two Federal Agents who look like they ate too many pasta salads and were ready to retire. The basement door was ajar, so he walked slowly towards it. He waited and listened for any footsteps or if he heard anyone talking. He pushed the door open slowly and peeked around inside to see if anyone or anything was in his way, stopping his clean get away. The basement was too dark for Martin to make out anything, so he took a big chance. No time to search for a light, he had been in the basement many of times before so he pretty much knew his way around. "Fuck" he yells as he hit his leg on something hard. He used he hands to move forward like a blind person. He felt a shelf, which he knew was close to the door which would lead him outside of his apartment building? His heart began to beat faster, he was just one step away from leaving his world behind and starting a new life somewhere no one knew him or his family. Two steps forward and his hands found the door. A smile crossed his face as his hands slid down the door to the handle. A noise, he looked up quickly. He thought he heard something coming from the stairwell. Nervously he stood still watching and waiting in the darkness. He tried to focus his eyes so he could see better in the darkness but it only made things worse. With his future so close to him,* he turned the doorknob, pushed the door open and ran. Looking back to see if anyone was running after him, he never seen who was right there before him. Martin had his eyes on the basement door and his mind on his getaway. As if he ran into a brick wall, Martin fell into darkness once more.

The Baldhead Murderer

Coming soon...

Made in the USA
Lexington, KY
22 March 2015